# Do Big Things:
# IN PORTUGAL

## Michael Kinney

I want to give a huge thanks to the following people for helping me with designs, editing, helpful advice and just someone to shoot ideas off when I thought I was going to throw in the towel and move to Alaska to start a commune. Instead, going through this process has taught me more than I expected.

- Mrs. Linda King (Mother and Inspiration)
- Kyle Phillips
- Katie Johnson
- Joshua Gateley
- Jesse James Davidson

Words & Photos: Michael Kinney
Publisher: Michael Kinney Media

ISBN: 979-8-218-49296-0

**<u>CONTACT INFORMATION</u>**

Website: MichaelKinneyMedia.com Photography/Prints:
MichaelKinney.smugmug.com IG, X: MkinneyMedia

# Contents


Forward    5

Chapter 1: Introduction: Why Do Big Things?    7

Chapter 2: Lisbon Yellow Line    23

Chapter 3: Food is Culture    32

Chapter 4: Religion & History    41

Chapter 5: The Tour Guide    60

Chapter 6: The People of Portugal    68

Chapter 7: Seeing Portugal    82

Chapter 8: Portugal in Blue    96

Chapter 9: MKM in Portugal    104

This book is dedicated to my niece, Alyssa:

"I want her to remember to not be afraid
to do the big (& difficult) things."

# Forward

Growing up in Lawton, Oklahoma, I was like most young boys. I had dramatic dreams of playing football at the University of Oklahoma and making a career with the Dallas Cowboys in the NFL.

This was my plan, and I wasn't even considering any backup options unless the Los Angeles Lakers needed a point guard.

Sadly, that was the breadth of my ambitions. If it wasn't sports-related or took place in the United States, my interest in it was minimal, to say the least. Unfortunately, that was the norm and not the exception.

However, once I realized in high school there wouldn't be too many openings for a 5-foot-7 offensive lineman on most teams in the NFL, I had to look for alternatives.

While attending Southwest Baptist University and playing football for the Bearcats, I searched for what other skill sets I could use to make my way in the world.

What came out of the search was me delving deep into the world of media. What started as just an interest in sports reporting turned into more than 20 years of working in all areas of journalism.

From business exposés to celebrity profiles to photography, I learned every facet of producing media content. I've written for various newspapers, magazines and websites around the country on a variety of different topics outside of sports.

I discovered I could connect those same skill sets with my growing passion for traveling. I started chronicling my work trips to places like New York City, Washington D.C., and Los Angeles. However, I quickly realized I wanted to do more and see more of the world I had ignored for so long. In other words, "Do Big Things".

That is where this book comes into play. It's my first foray into international travel in which the sole mission of the trip was to document my experiences through writing and photography.

Do Big Things is my attempt to show people that there is no need to fear the world outside your door. To open yourself up to new experiences and to go do big things in new places.

Doing big things doesn't necessarily just mean traveling to the other side of the world to climb Mount Kilimanjaro or catching the waves at Nazare Beach where the swells can reach 100 feet. It could encompass learning a new language, starting a new business or even working on a book when everyone says no one buys them anymore.

Overcoming the doubts and fears that have kept you from doing something that could be life-changing is the very definition of Doing Big Things. That is what this project has been for me.

Thank you for deciding to take this journey with me.

*Michael Kinney*

# Chapter 1

# Introduction:
# Why Do Big Things?

On Nov. 1, 1755, the city of Lisbon, Portugal was nearly destroyed. A series of devastating earthquakes that are believed to have registered as high as 9.0 leveled the capital of Portugal.

The quake was so violent, it generated a tsunami with 20-foot high waves that crashed into the port city as well. At that point, the future of Lisbon was in doubt at what had become known as the "Great Lisbon Earthquake."

Almost three centuries later, not only has Lisbon been rebuilt, but it has also become a popular tourist destination in Europe.

When I first started planning for my first Do Big Things trip in 2023, I chose Portugal because I knew little to nothing about the country. Besides it being in Europe and its long history with the Atlantic slave trade, it was a blank page to me.

So, while most travelers to Europe were heading to Paris, Rome or Munich, I touched down in Lisbon with no plan, no real itinerary and no preconceived idea of what the next 10 days had in store for me.

What you will see over the span of 64 pages is a look at a country whose known history stretches back to at least 45 B.C. when it was incorporated into the Roman Republic.

Yet, Portugal is going through a transformation. No longer seen as the forgotten stepchild of Europe, Portugal is evolving (or devolving depending on POV) into a tourist destination. Castles that are centuries old have been turned into popular Airbnbs (Castle of Óbidos), ride-sharing apps (Uber, Bolt) have begun to replace the iconic tram system for locals, and McDonald's and Starbucks can now be found in small seaside towns like Cascais. In 2024 it was voted the 5th safest European country to visit by the Global Peace Index.

For the residents of cities like Lisbon, Porta, the Douro Valley and Sintra, this emphasis on tourism means more international money flowing into their economy. But they are left to question at what cost.

The old-world charm is still evident when walking on the Mosaic cobblestone streets in neighborhoods like Alfama or when taking a sunset cruise on a small fishing boat through the Mediterranean.

This book is meant to be more than an interesting collection of travel photography. It is a journey seen through inquisitive eyes as I visited a variety of different spots. From the popular destinations (Lisbon, Porto, Nazaré) to the overlooked locales (Fatima, Obidos, Batalha), this photographic trip is of a country with one foot anchored in the past and eyes gazing toward an uncertain future.

---

## **Cutline:**

On the following page: Despite the choppy waters along the Portugal coastline, a fisherman was up early looking for that first bite of the day. This may have been my favorite photo cap-tured from the entire trip because it not only says something about the Portuguese people, it's also familiar to nearly every culture around the world. This print and others from my travels can be found at MichaelKinney.Smugmug.com.

GELATO & CAFFE
S PERFEITOS
14 DEZEMBRO
NOS CINEMAS

MUSEU
FRESS
MUSEU

zona
10

# Chapter 2

# Lisbon Yellow Line

By Michael Kinney

In 1755, Lisbon began a new path in history with the "Great Lisbon Earthquake."

Almost three centuries after the quake, not only has Lisbon been rebuilt, it has become a popular destination for tourists from around the world. In 2023 more than 3.6 million visitors came to the city.

At some point, nearly every one of those visitors likely found themselves riding on Lisbon's iconic bright yellow trams (streetcar or trolley) that maneuver through the same streets that had once been turned to rubble.

While in Lisbon I stayed in the historic Alfama district, I rode the trams and got a feel for just what makes them special

Despite the majestic views and historic architecture that attract tourists to Lisbon, it has been the bright yellow trams that have become the symbol of the city. They are featured in movies, TV shows, paintings and popular postcards that are sent around the world.

Go anywhere in Lisbon, at almost any time of the day or night, and you're bound to see a tram cross your path. From 6 a.m. when they first start their routes until past midnight, they can be seen gliding slowly through the colorful mosaic of cobblestone that makes up the narrow, winding paths – which can at times feel more like a maze than a network of streets – in a major city.

Lisbon (also called Lisboa by the Portuguese) is currently just one of three cities in Portugal – along with Porto and Sintra – to continue use of the trams, and the only one to keep them as a vital part of its public transportation system.

"Trams in Porto are only for sightseeing, while in Lisbon they are a local transportation mode," said a resident of Lisbon. "But we also have touristic trams in Lisbon. The Tram 28 in Lisbon is the more famous one, and I strongly recommend taking it as early as possible – until 9 a.m. You should be considerate to locals, especially older people and families with young children."

The electric tram didn't make its appearance in Lisbon until 1901, but it had a progenitor: The first tramway was a horsecar line in 1873 by Carris. At that time, the vehicles were called "Carros Americanos" because the idea came from America. However, they were unable to traverse the steep hills and rocky roads in areas like Alfama, until they switched to cable cars in 1884. The first electric tram, which went into operation at the dawn of the 20th century, carried passengers from Cais do Sodré to Algés, a distance of just under 10 km.

The Lisbon tramway network is still owned and operated by the Carris company. Many of its carriages are easily recognizable by the bright yellow that can be found on the celebrated Tram 28, which covers the areas from Martim Moniz Square to Campo de Ourique and takes passengers through Alfama past the historical sites.

"I was in Alfama at the starting point of route 28," said one tourist, who recently visited Lisbon in 2023. "The lineup was epic. I enjoyed watching trams drive past and taking photos of them with cool urban backgrounds."

There are five other lines, and one ride costs 3 euros for a ticket, which can be purchased from the driver. In total, the network in Lisbon spans 19 miles and consists of 63 trams in operation. Of those, 45 are considered historic remodelado (remodels), made to look and feel just as they were a century ago.

The trams work in conjunction with other public transportation such as the bus, the railroads and the subways. Tourists are encouraged to purchase the Lisbon or Viva Viagem cards, which can be used on all forms of public transportation and offer a less expensive rate.

Yet, this has also become an issue for those like Pedro Pinheiro Vaz, who was born and raised in Lisbon.

"It would be fantastic if people could think of them as public transportation — because that's what they are — and not just another tourist attraction," Vaz said. "Locals gave up long ago on waiting in line for hours to get on a precious means of transportation that could be really useful for people who live in the city."

Despite those waits, the future of the tram could be on shaky ground. As ride-sharing apps continue to proliferate throughout the region, and people become in more of a hurry to see all that Portugal has to offer, it has become seen as a relic of a bygone past.

But that is also what makes the tram so appealing to visitors and residents alike. It's a reminder of when people weren't in such a hurry and there was time to hold a conversation or watch a sunset while looking out the window of the tram rather than down at a cell phone.

"In Lisbon, we rode Tram 12 from Martim Moniz since there was no line," said another visitor to Portugal. "Later in the day we got on Tram 28 near Estrela and rode back to Martim Moniz and also avoided any lines. All were fun and enjoyable."

carris
Coca-Cola
Real Magic
O MUNDO PRECISA DE
MAIS PAIS NATAIS
DE
SÃO TOMÉ
66
JOGOS
SANTACASA
KO

CARREIRA Nº
579
Coca-Cola
Real Magic

Partidas
Departures
Infraestruturas
de Portugal
HORA   DESTINO   LINHA COMBOIO   OPER   OBSERVAÇÕES
Chegadas
Arrivals
Infraestruturas
de Portugal
HORA   ORIGEM   LINHA COMBOIO   OPER   OBSERVAÇÕES
CP

548
WI-FI

# Chapter 3

# Food is Culture

By Michael Kinney

One of the great things about being able to travel and see different parts of the world is feasting on local cuisine.

When I started to plan a December trip to Portugal and Spain, one of the first things

I investigated was the types of food I would come face to face with. Right off the bat, I realized that despite their location in Europe, the two neighbors not only had different diets from each other, but they also had varying tastes within their own borders.

This excited me but also presented a challenge. I didn't want to say I had one meal in Lisbon and try to say to represented Sintra or the beach town Cascia. The same went for Spain.

So I chose to take one single solitary dish and one dish only from each area I visited. For better or worse that single dish was going to stand on business by itself be the face of an entire region/city.

I will publish a few different reviews over the next few weeks that focus on one dish. I am starting with the iconic Francesinha.

On my third day in Portugal, I made a quick day trip over to Porto. It was close enough (1 hour) and cheap enough ($47) to hop on a flight and be there before the sun had fully risen.

I sent out the bat signal for a Bolt, the European version of Uber and Lyft, and had them take me to Livraria Lello: The World's Most Beautiful Bookstore (actual name). On the ride over I asked the driver what is one local food I need to try while I am in town. Without hesitation, he blurted out Francesinha (Little French Woman).

He then proceeded to give me a breakdown of why even though the Francesinha can be found throughout the country, the original version was created in Porto and only they do it right.

So, after a long day exploring, I began to look for a place to eat along a busy and crowded Porto Port.

Almost every restaurant had a sign that stated they served Francesinha. But either the lines were too long or they were set up to look like an American beach diner. I finally found a spot near the end of the boardwalk that was run by an old Portuguese couple who seemed to be exasperated every time I asked a question. I figured if anybody knew how to make an authentic Francesinha, it would have to be them.

What they brought back startled me. In fact, I was scared.

Recipes vary depending on where you eat in Porto but generally, it includes steak, sausage, and ham just for starters. There were two other pieces of meat that I couldn't make out right away and it was all stuffed between thick slices of white bread.

But what gives it its unique look is that it is drenched with melted cheese, blistering hot tomato sauce, and sometimes beer. It then can be topped with a sunny-side-up egg.

It looked like something a college frat student would put together after a hard night of drinking and rejection.

But as bad as it looked, it tasted even worse. None of the meats made sense together. I was in total shock when on my fourth bite I realized one of the ingredients was a hot dog.

This was also when I came to realize, the idea of seasoning has not made its way to Europe yet. With no salt, pepper or paprika to be found, I couldn't even mask the taste or pretend it was something else. It stood on business (my new favorite saying) by itself.

The Francesinha's one redeeming quality is that it was filling. Despite not finishing the entire meal, I didn't eat the rest of the day.

So, while I can't envision myself ever ordering the Francesinha ever again, I will give it a slight pass due to the price ($14) and its ability to sustain a person for an entire day. But it is a very small pass since I really do have a hard rule about enjoying my food.

Yet, while it wasn't high on taste, I still gave the experience high marks. That's because I tried something new. I didn't hesitate to step outside my world of burgers, pizza and chicken sandwiches to experience something new.

While this attempt didn't go as planned, there were other times during the trip when

I devoured some amazing cuisines. At the end of each day, I will carry the memory of experiencing new cultures more than an upset palette.

BACALHAU
PIZZAS
LASANHA
SANDWICHES
SALADAS
PANADOS
*
DOCES CASEIROS

...stanhas
Chestnuts
3€ / duzia

EM QUER QUENTES E BOAS, QUENTINHAS?

ATM
Secure.Universal.Available.

ATM

Customer Service (+351) 214 201 9...

Express access to your money.
Anywhere. Anytime.

LISBOA
CÂMARA MUNICIPAL

A GINJINHA

O MATHEUS é um CHUCHINHA,
MAIS FEIO que um CAMAFEU,
MAGRO, TÍSICO, um FUINHA
NUNCA na VIDA BEBEU,
NEM um COPO de GINJINHA.

O IRMÃO que SADE e VIRTUDE,
NESTA DIVINA AMBROSIA,
É GORDO COMO um ALMUDE,
BEBE SEUS COPOS POR DIA,
POR ISSO GOSA SAUDE.

McDonald's

CAIXA AUTOMÁTICO
CASH DISPENSER
GELDAUTOMAT
CAJERO AUTOMÁTICO
RETRAIT

FRESH BAKED
HANDMADE
EMPANADAS
COCKTAILS * VINHOS * SMOOTHIES
MARGARITA * NEGRONI    ROSE * BRANCO    BANANA * MORANGO
FERNET COLA * FRENCH 5  INTO * VERDE    LIMÃO * MANGA
LARANJA * MELANCIA
FRESH
BAKED EMPANADAS HAND MADE
HOT

# Chapter 4

---

# Religion & History

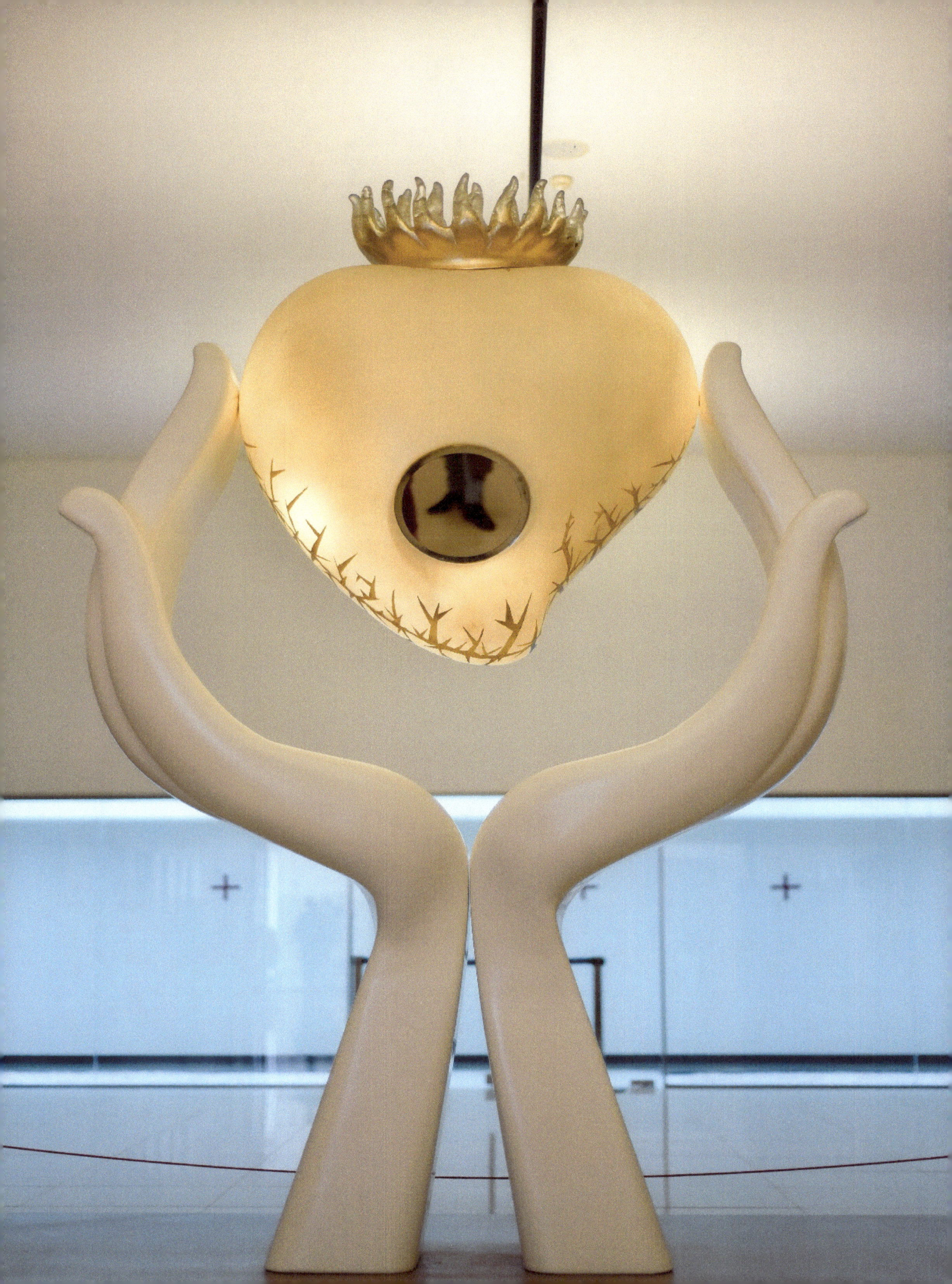

João Paulo II

ROSARIUM:
ALEGRIA E LUZ, DOR E GLÓRIA
— O ROSÁRIO COMO CAMINHO DA FÉ
S. PEDRO E S. PAULO

# SACRISTIA

REGINA SACRATISSIMI ROSARII FATIMÆ ORA PRO NOBIS

I.N.R.I

O CONDESTAVEL
NUNO ALVARES PEREIRA
1360-1431
ALJVBARROTA

S. VICENTE

# Chapter 5

# The Tour Guide

By Michael Kinney

When I first signed up for the Get Your Guide Tour, there were several locations I was excited to explore. None more than Nazaré beach. With its history of producing record-breaking waves and surfers who tried to ride them, I was hoping it was going to be my lucky day.

However, of all the places we were going to hit during the nine-hour tour, the one I had the least excitement for was Fatima. In fact, when I initially signed up, I had no idea why a town with 13,000 residents was even important. In my mind, It was just one stop I had to endure before getting to see the giant waves.

It was our small group tour guide, Carlos (Not his real name), who first hinted that Fatima was going to be something special. I didn't know anyone else in our eight-person tour and I was only one of two Americans, so I couldn't give anyone a look of disbelief or a sarcastic side eye when he made this statement.

However, Carlos turned out to be right, but not for the reasons he thought.

Fatima, which gets more than 8 million visitors each year, is home to the Sanctuary of Fátima. It is best known for its tale of the Miracle of Fatima, which Carlos knew by heart.

At first, I thought it was because he had given the tour hundreds, maybe thousands of times.

But, it was when Carlos started to give more philosophical answers to questions about the sanctuary and its traditions that we found out he was doling out more than just the normal tour guide info.

Carlos said he had grown up believing he was going to be a priest in the Catholic church. He attended seminary school and at one point had been on the verge of taking his vows to complete the transition.

However, at the last moment, Carlos said he had a crisis of conscious and was unable to take the vows. While he was still an ardent believer in the faith and the church, parts of the Catholic doctrine and traditions had turned him away.

Carlos went on to travel the world and work in all manner of different jobs and professions until he found his way back home and became a tour guide. He admitted the church was still an important part of his life.

This became apparent at the Sanctuary of Our Lady of Fatima. As we headed toward the Basilica de Nossa Senhora do Rosário, which holds Mass each day, a long and direct white path stood out. It led from the sanctuary to the Chapel of Apparitions, where Catholics can light a candle to pray, set an intention or honor someone who has passed.

People were crawling along the path on all fours or on their knees as they clasped Rosary beads.

Carlos explained that this was a form of penance they had chosen to take on. Called the Way of The Penance, similar pilgrimages are made at the Vatican in Rome.

"Millions of pilgrims come to Fatima each year to pray and do penance, obeying the Mother of God's urgent request for prayer, sacrifice and reparation," according to The Fatima Center. "Here we see pilgrims on the Via Sacra, the principal street of Fatima which begins in the Cova da Iria and terminates in a garden near the Cabeço."

All of this takes place as tourists, like me, are walking past them, staring and getting content for social media.

It was obvious Carlos had conflicting feelings and thoughts about the practice of paying penance as he explained its purpose to us.

But what made me do a double-take was when we spotted a woman, probably in her 60s, all alone and crawling along the path. Not even halfway to the Chapel of Apparitions, she was struggling.

As our group stared uncomfortably at her and I took photos, Carlos walked over to her and conversed for a few minutes before giving what appeared to be a Catholic absolution prayer.

When Carlos came back to our group and explained why he made such a gesture, the inner conflict could once again be heard in his voice. He pitied her, but at the same time understood her faith.

This is a scene that plays out every day, six times a week for Carlos. I can't imagine the feelings and emotions he must feel each time he guides a group and has to explain the life he basically turned away from.

Carlos was just as informative at stops in Batalha, Nazaré and Óbidos. He knew his history and culture and provided entertaining tales and historical nuggets everywhere we went. He even told me the right dessert to eat when at a restaurant on Nazaré Beach.

But it was that little exchange between him and a suffering woman that stayed with me throughout the rest of the tour. Still not entirely sure why and it will be something I will ruminate on for some time.

Carlos went down as one of the most interesting people I met throughout my stay in Portugal.

In fact, each of the tours I took were led by some fascinating individuals with a varied and rich history.

Hugo is a boat captain who took me on a Sunset tour I found through Airbnb experiences. But he was also a connoisseur of food throughout Europe and had a deep knowledge of Portuguese history and nautical lore.

My walking tour through the streets of Lisbon, which was also an Airbnb experience, was fronted by Samuel. He provided a more nuanced understanding of what Lisbon is today and what it used to be. The former student had held similar occupations in Spain and other parts of Europe.

They all gave me a new appreciation for the tour guide profession. In the future, it will be impossible for me to not ask as many questions about their lives as I do about the tour itself.

# Chapter 6

## The People of Portugal

drinks
&
lifestyle

VICTOR da COSTA PEREIRA
nascido 1919
2013
O Senhor mais velho do Bairro
Fundador Grupo Desportivo Mouraria
Orgulho pelo seu Bairro
Que viu tanta coisa bonita e boa

PASTELARIA

Partidas
Departures

Infraestruturas
de Portugal

| HORA | DESTINO | LINHA | COMBOIO | OPER | OBSERVAÇÕES |

Chegadas
Arrivals

Infraestruturas
de Portugal

| HORA | ORIGEM | LINHA | COMBOIO | OPER | OBSERVAÇÕES |

# Chapter 7

# Seeing Portugal

LELLO & IRMÃO

144

LIVRARIA
CHARDRON

LIVRARIA LELLO

PALESTINA
LIVRE

63

FARMÁCIA

MORÃO
HERDEIROS

FARMÁCIA MORÃO

DECUS
IN
LABO
RE

SUPER BOCK
DELTA
O CAFÉ DA SUA VIDA
SUPER BOCK

MUSE
da vil
TOWN MUSE
USEU
ila
MUSEUM
CASCAIS

- 95 -

# Chapter 8

## Portugal in Blue

LISBOA

4 A
AL

7

PASSEIO
CARLOS ANDRADE
TEIXEIRA
( JORNALISTA )

CARMO

# Chapter 9

---

# MKM in Portugal

MKM
MICHAEL KINNEY MEDIA

MKM
MICHAEL KINNEY MEDIA